RAIN FOREST BABIES

PARROT CHICKS

by Genevieve Nilsen

I0794105

TABLE OF CONTENTS

tadpole books

WORDS TO KNOW

chicks

feeds

fly

mom

rain forest

trees

PARROT CHICKS

These are parrot chicks!

They live in the rain forest.

They live in trees.

Mom feeds them.

They grow up.

They can be many colors.

feathers

These are blue.

These are red.

They fly!

Pretty!

LET'S REVIEW!

What colors are these parrots?

INDEX